Alexander Hamilton

A biography of Alexander Hamilton, one of America's founding fathers

Table of Contents

Introduction

Thank you for taking the time to pick up this book about Alexander Hamilton.

This book serves as a biography of Alexander Hamilton, one of America's founding fathers.

In the following chapters you will learn all about Alexander Hamilton's incredible life, including how he emerged from humble beginnings to an ultimate position of power in the government.

This book details Hamilton's many contributions to the development of the United States, as well as the scandals and controversies he was involved in throughout his career.

At the completion of this book you will have a good understanding of the amazing life that Alexander Hamilton lived, and have a true appreciation for the incredible impact he had on our political and legal systems.

Once again, thanks for taking the time to read this book, I hope you find it to be helpful!

Chapter One: The Background of Alexander Hamilton

Alexander Hamilton was one of the most influential people the United States has ever seen. He is one of the Founding Fathers, and had a massive voice in the United States Government's political system, as well as its Treasury. But, his life also included various scandals, arguments, and war-time experiences that shaped him into the man that we would eventually see rise from the ashes, before being shot to death in a duel against Burr.

Alexander Hamilton was born in Charlestown, British West Indies, to Rachel Faucette and James A. Hamilton. He was born out of wedlock and was eventually orphaned as a child by his mother's death and his father's incompetence and abandonment. He ended up being taken in by an older cousin who eventually gave him over to a prosperous merchant family who could take care of him in ways his cousin would never have been able to. As he grew, he was recognized for his intelligence and talent, and was eventually sponsored by a group of rich local men to travel to New York City to pursue his education. Hamilton attended King's College and ended up staying to create and seek out his fortune.

Alexander Hamilton spent part of his childhood in Charlestown, which is the capital of the island of Nevis in the Leeward Islands. Hamilton and his older brother, James Jr., were both born out of wedlock, and there was much speculation and rumor in the community that Hamilton's mother was of a mixed race. However, the claim lacked verifiable evidence, and to this day is believed to simply be a rumor started by what scholars can only assume were women whispering about the Hamilton family. Being born out of wedlock was an absolute scandal, and for Hamilton, it would foreshadow the rest of his life and the outcome of the paths he chose to take.

Interestingly, no one is sure whether Hamilton was born in 1755 or 1757. Much of the historical evidence after Hamilton's arrival to the Thirteen Colonies supports the idea that he was born in 1757, including self-proclamation within Hamilton's own writings. Hamilton listed his birth year as 1757 when he first arrived and celebrated his birthdays on January 11th. This proved as much evidence as historians would need until around 1930 when additional conflicting documentation of his early life in the Caribbean was published.

A probate paper from St. Croix in 1768 that was created after the death of Hamilton's mother actually listed him as 13 years old. The issue with that age is that, when calculated backwards, it actually puts his birth year as 1755. Historians have since speculated on the possible reasons that could have accounted for two different years of birth to have appeared in multiple historical documents. If 1755 is the correct year, Hamilton might have been trying to appear younger while he was in college so as to not stand out by being older than his classmates. This theory is the most prevailing one.

However, if 1757 is his correct birth year, the probate document (which is the only document that has this particular birth year on it) may have simply included an error. Other swirling theories around this idea are that Hamilton might have given his age as 13 after his mother's death in an attempt to appear more employable so that he could still have a way of taking care of himself and his family. Historians have since found that this probate document harbored other proven wrongs within its paperwork, rendering the document unreliable in terms of historical accuracy.

His mother, while still alive, had been married to multiple men, including Hamilton's father, and that would eventually catch up to her later in life and after her death. James

Hamilton abandoned Rachel Faucette and their sons to save her from a charge of bigamy, seeing as she was still married to her previous husband legally while initiating a marriage proposal with James. After both of those divorces, she supported her children in St. Croix and kept a small store in Christiansted that helped put food on the table and keep clothes on the backs of her children. Eventually, she contracted a bad fever and died on February 19, 1768. Within the questionable documents of the probate court, Faucette's first husband, still angry from the sting of desertion, claimed her estate and took off with the few valuables she had owned. The items he didn't take were auctioned off, and a friend took pity on Hamilton's fragile state by purchasing the family's books for Hamilton.

As Hamilton grew up, he became a clerk at local import-export firm called *Beekman and Cruger*, who traded specifically with New England. He was left in charge of the firm for five months while the owner was at sea, and that earned him great credibility within the industry that he carried with him throughout his life. Him and his brother were taken in briefly by their cousin Peter Lytton, who ultimately committed suicide. With the emotional turmoil that the two brothers had experienced together, it rifted their relationship and they eventually separated. James took up an apprenticeship with a local carpenter while Alexander was given a home by Nevis merchant Thomas Stevens. There were rumors that swallowed Hamilton's story whole, like the fact that Thomas Stevens was actually Alexander's biological father, though there is no evidence to support that fact.

Hamilton continued clerking and remained an avid reader who later developed an interest in writing. He began to dream of a life outside the island where he lived, and he wrote a letter to his father that housed a detailed account of a hurricane that had devastated the island. This is considered the first ever publication that Hamilton ever wrote because Hugh Knox, who was a minister and journalist, ended up publishing the letter in the *Royal Danish-American Gazette*. This is the moment that impressed the community leaders so much that it spurred them to collect a fund to send Hamilton to the colonies for his education.

But, just as Hamilton's childhood was as tumultuous as the waves of a storm, his education was no different. The Church of England ended up denying membership to both Alexander and James Hamilton, Jr., as well as education within their church schools, because they were born out of wedlock. They ended up receiving individual tutoring and classes in a private school. Hamilton wouldn't let the setback stop him from learning absolutely everything he could, and he supplemented his education with the family library of 34 books.

In October 1772, he finally arrived on the mainland and began learning the fundamental subjects missing from his education. He understood that his family library lacked viable information necessary for his life, and so he sought out other ways to be educated in this new land he had stepped upon. He attended the Elizabethtown Academy and studied with Francis Barber in preparation for his college work. He found the influence of William Livingston (who he would live with for a time), and he would individually study as much as he could until he finally entered The King's College in New York City. He entered in the fall semester of 1773 as a private student and officially enrolled as a regular student in May 1774. His friend, Robert Troup, spoke highly and boasted of Hamilton's ability to clearly and concisely explain his thoughts and ideas, including the rights and reasons that patriots had in their case against the British. But his influence didn't stop there. Hamilton, Troup, and four other undergraduates formed an unnamed literary society that is widely recognized as the precursor to the Philolexian Society.

Hamilton's political writings took off in 1774, when he began responding anonymously to Samuel Seabury's pamphlets that he was publishing on the Loyalist cause. Entitled *A Full*

Vindication of the Measures of Congress and *The Farmer Refuted,* these became known as Hamilton's first political writings. Hamilton was a supporter of the Revolutionary cause, even at this pre-war stage, but he didn't approve of mob reprisals against Loyalists. He wholly and completely believed that you could get your point across without violence or outright acts of vandalism, which completely juxtaposes his future involvement within the American Revolutionary War.

Hamilton was eventually forced to discontinue his studies before graduating because the college closed its doors while the British occupied the city. When the war finally ended, Hamilton passed the Bar exam after many months of self-study and was licensed to argue cases before the Supreme Court of the State of New York. Then, while Hamilton was stationed in Morristown, New Jersey, he met Elizabeth Schuyler. She was a daughter of General Philip Schuyler and Catherine Van Rensselaer, and the two were married on December 14, 1780. The had eight children together, and never once divorced.

Chapter Two: The Emerging of Hamilton's Political Views

Alexander Hamilton was among many individuals that were unsatisfied with the weak national government. He led the Annapolis Convention, which successfully gained enough ground to make Congress call for the drafting of a new constitution. Hamilton was a hearty and active participant through its entire drafting and ratification process, and he helped achieve the constitution's ratification by writing 51 of the 85 installments of *The Federalist Papers*. To this day, those installments are the single most important reference for the interpretation of the United States Constitution.

Hamilton is an enigma. Both modern day parties claim him as being on their side, and they aren't wrong. In his writings, support for both sides can be wholly and completely seen and stated. Hamilton wanted to expand the national government, whereas Jefferson and those that opposed his views wanted the government to keep a low profile. He believed in the freedom of the press, made evident by when he argued the Zenger case and promoted the idea of a National Bank to stabilize the currency, and he also believed in the government completely paying off its debts. He believed that protective tariffs would allow American business to grow despite the fact that it made imported goods higher priced. His adversary, Jefferson, was completely opposed to many of these ideals and stated that these policies benefited the already-wealthy at the expense of small farmers. Back then, the party that he officially belonged to was call the Federalist Party.

Sounds like a familiar fight, doesn't it?

Hamilton's views were a little of both sides, and their roots can be seen in the work that he did for the government, as well as after his resignation in 1795.

Hamilton found himself as the leading cabinet member within this new government under President George Washington. Hamilton emphasized a strong central government, and successfully debated that the implied powers of the new Constitution provided higher Treasury authority, and ended up creating the government-backed Bank of the United States. These programs were funded primarily by tariffs on imports, and later by a highly controversial tax on whiskey that Hamilton would impose simply to anger people.

To overcome the local ideas that suppressed Hamilton's voice, he ended up mobilizing a nationwide network that would eventually become the Federalist Party. But, here was the massive issue with an American two-party system: The Jay Treaty. This treaty established friendly trade relations with Britain, which didn't sit well with the supporters of the French Revolution. Hamilton had a central role in the Federalist party, and it was the party that dominated politics until it lost the election of 1800 to Jefferson's Democratic-Republican Party with the help of Hamilton himself! Apparently, the only person more disgusting to him than Jefferson was Aaron Burr, the man who would end up killing Hamilton in his old age.

After the Battle of Yorktown in 1781, Hamilton resigned his commission from the Continental Army. He was soon appointed in July 1782 to the Congress of the Confederation as a New York State representative, and he made sure to take the criticisms he had written about long before he had been appointed to Congress along with him. In one of these critical letters he wrote, "The fundamental defect is a want of power in Congress...the confederation itself is defective and requires to be altered; it is neither fit for war, nor peace." He understood that the system was severely broken, but little did he know the impact he would actually have in attempting to fix it.

An amendment to the Articles had been proposed just before Hamilton's appointment by Thomas Burke that would give Congress the authority to collect a 5% duty on all imports.

However, this required the agreement of all of the states, and Rhode Island continued to reject it. So, being the financial mind that Hamilton was, he persuaded Congress to send a group out to persuade the entity of Rhode Island to change its mind. While things didn't quite go according to plan because of Virginia eventually backing out of their agreement as well, this was a massive step to proving Hamilton's worth and influence as the future Secretary of the Treasury.

In 1784, he founded the Bank of New York, further proving his passion and dedication for financial stability on all accounts. This bank would become one of the longest operating banks in American history, and it stayed in business for over 220 years before its merger with another bank in 2007. Hamilton had been frustrated for quite some time with the weak Articles of Confederation, so he had a hand in drafting its resolution for a constitutional convention. In doing so, it brought his longtime belief to life: to have a more powerful and more financially independent government.

In September 1789, Hamilton was elected Secretary of the Treasury under President George Washington. While on his staff, Hamilton became frustrated with the decentralized nature of the government and spat at its dependency upon its own states for financial support. Under the Articles of Confederation, Hamilton knew that Congress had no power to collect taxes or demand money from the states, and he scoffed at the lack of stable funding that made it difficult for its Army to obtain its necessities. They couldn't even properly pay their soldiers! Hamilton was absolutely astounded, and he set out to change it.

In 1795, after his resignation from Secretary of the Treasury, Hamilton returned to New York to practice law. He tried to control the policies of President Adams by becoming chummy with him, and in 1798, Hamilton called for mobilization against France after the XYZ Affair. This entire debacle, complete with an undeclared war called the Quasi-War, was nothing more than a pumped-up standoff between two different parts of the world. However, in order to avoid the issues at sea slowly finding their way to land, President Adams found a solution that avoided a war with France.

Hamilton continued his legal and personal business ventures in New York City, and was an active presence in ending the international slave trade. He found slavery to be absolutely deplorable, and he even worked during the Revolutionary War to train black people who wanted to fight. Hamilton would eventually rally against Vice President Burr when he ran for governor of New York in 1804, and Burr's personal offense at the matter would be what spurred the duel that would mortally wound Hamilton.

Hamilton has been seen as the Father of American Economics. This philosophy dominated economic policy after 1861. Among the ideals of this philosophy are Hamilton's core beliefs on finances: supporting government intervention in favor of business and opposition to the British definition of free trade. In Hamilton's eyes, a strong executive government could become the linchpin of an administrative republic if linked to the support of the people. In other words, a strong executive government could aid in the strict organization of political matters and bureaucracy as long as it was always done with the best of its people in mind. Hamilton felt that the dominance of executive leadership along with successfully carrying out policy was necessary to resist deterioration of the newly-budding republican government.

Back during Hamilton's time, many people considered his ideals of money and the way the government should work elitist, and maybe they still are. Hamilton, among other things, wanted to fund the federal debt at face value, which ultimately saved the budding government from plunging into financial chaos and ruin after the Revolution. Alongside the many accomplishments born out of his mind and his determination, his Report on Manufactures helped to foster commercial and industrial development throughout the new nation. While his ideas of government straddled the fence at times, his ideals behind his financial plans and his outlook on economics never wavered with the times. He knew exactly what he felt the government should do financially in order to balance itself out and not be dependent on the states for financial support, and he made sure that he fixed and educated as much as he could while he was still in office.

While it is said that Hamilton's religious beliefs were strong in his youth, it has been rumored that as he found his head for government that he lost his heart for religion. It has been stated and recorded that Hamilton would make jokes as religion's expense while simultaneously proclaiming that he was a man of religion. However, it can be found in many of his documents that Hamilton frequently used religion to both justify and shoot down various ideals, as well as his own changing and emerging ideals, whenever he found it necessary. Nevertheless, his sound financial principles within his time of governmental serving laid the foundation for various philosophies, policies, and outlooks that we still have today. No matter his religious affiliations, Alexander Hamilton influenced history beyond what he could have probably foreseen himself, and it's all thanks to his financially-guided opinions and outlook.

Chapter Three: The Jefferson Feud

The feud between Alexander Hamilton and Thomas Jefferson is one of the first great rivalries of our nation's history. Hamilton, leader of the Federalists, and Jefferson, leader of the Anti-Federalists, were constantly trying to undo one another. Being the leaders of opposing parties is feud enough, but their feud was much deeper, and much longer, than just the length and depth of the parties. Everything about what the two believed was in opposition with the other, and the clash over Hamilton's national bank would solidify their rivalry in history.

The fight between Hamilton and Jefferson was less about their difference in personalities (though they were exact opposites there, as well) than it was about competing ideals and theories of government. Jefferson saw a government that was strong and centralized on foreign policy, but was hands-off and incredibly restrained on its own domestic matters. Jefferson was always suspicious of anything that compromised individual self-sufficiency (after all, the man even hated the basic outline of a city!) and was horrified at the thought of Americans depending on their government for provision in their life. He always believed that a citizen dependent on the government couldn't be independent, and that it spelled disaster in the long-run for any society attempting to build itself up. To Jefferson, it meant that the government had compromised individual private life so much so that self-sustainable life was no longer achievable.

However, this was what Hamilton believed should happen, and he had hopes to use the Treasury to make his vision a reality. Hamilton believed that the government was required to play a massive role in the lives of its citizens, and that consolidated national identity should be primary. By issuing huge amounts of debt and allowing people to borrow money to pay back in increments at a later time, he hoped to involve the Treasury in the day-to-day operations of the economy.

The two drastically different ideals of government of boasted of two strictly different understandings of American power and the American people. For Hamilton, America's strength was within its commerce. Hamilton's America was filled with businessmen and entrepreneurs, as well as bankers and those knowledgeable on finances. He wanted to see America competing heavily in the global marketplace, and he felt that the only way to do that was to use the government.

Jefferson, of course, vehemently disagreed with Hamilton about the basic makeup of the American people. He believed that the people working for Hamilton were just in it for themselves, and that the government had no responsibility to help people who were already well off. Jefferson felt that, if anything, the government should be helping farmers that were constantly preyed upon. In Jefferson's eyes, the best way to help those farmers was to leave the actual power close to them in their state governments and to keep the federal government out of the way. His fight with Hamilton, through his eyes, was a disagreement about who should rule in the name of the people: Hamilton believed in the few, and Jefferson believed in the many.

During Hamilton's years as Secretary of the Treasury, political parties and factions began to emerge. A Congressional caucus began as an opposition group to Hamilton's financial programs, and Thomas Jefferson ultimately joined this group. Hamilton and his allies began to call themselves Federalists while the opposing group called themselves the Anti-Federalists. Their name would eventually be changed to the Republican Party. Here, the rivalry began with just a clash of beliefs on how much control the central government should have and what kind of dictation they should have over the states.

Hamilton assembled supporters nationwide to support his political party as well as the expansive financial programs. He wanted to garner support for the president's policy of neutrality during the European war between Britain and France, and he wanted to gain steam in order to run over Jefferson's budding political faction. Hamilton's campaign attacked the French minister, Edmond-Charles Genêt, who had tried to influence voters directly. The Federalists claimed that this was foreign interference in American affairs, and that it should not be something that is allowed.

However, the Jeffersonian Republicans opposed banks and favored involvement on the side of France during the war. They built their own national movement to oppose the Federalists, and they quickly gained ground behind them. Both sides gained the support of local political factions, and each side ended up developing its own biased newspapers. The writers and editors for the Federalists were Noah Webster, John Fenno, and William Cobbett; and Benjamin Franklin Bache and Philip Freneau were the spunky Republican editors. All of these newspapers and writings were characterized by fiery personal attacks, extreme exaggerations, and even completely invented claims, much like our current political commercials that run during our own voting years. In 1801, Hamilton would establish a daily newspaper entitled the *New York Evening Post*, and this newspaper would transcend history. It is still publishing today as the *New York Post*.

The intense feud between Hamilton and Jefferson is the best known and, historically, the most important in American political history. Their incompatibility was written in at the basis of their beliefs and values as individual men, but it was only heightened by their conglomerate shared wish to be Washington's principal and most trusted advisor.

There was an early clash between them that occurred shortly after Jefferson took office as Secretary of State in 1790, and it led to an important interpretation of the Constitution. When Hamilton introduced his bill as Secretary of the Treasury to establish a national bank, Jefferson argued that the Constitution clearly expressed all the powers belonging to the federal government and, out of assumption, reserved all other powers to the states. Jefferson's argument (that was seen through the eyes of people who only cared about states' rights) is that nowhere was it explicitly stated that the federal government was empowered to set up a bank.

Hamilton quickly responded that because of the mass of necessary detail and general clauses that one of these clauses applied, and it was the one that authorized Congress to "make all laws which shall be necessary and proper" for carrying out other powers specifically granted. Hamilton stated that the Constitution authorized the national government to impose and collect taxes, pay its debts, as well as borrow money. His argument was that a national bank would fundamentally help in performing these specific functions more efficiently. Keeping on with his rebuttal, Congress was, therefore, entitled under its implied powers to create the bank. Washington and Congress would eventually accept Hamilton's view and set an overtly important precedent for the expansive interpretation of the federal government's authority.

However, despite their feud, the phrase "the enemy of my enemy is my friend" came to prevail between the two of them when Thomas Jefferson and Aaron Burr decided to run for president on the same party ticket. Hamilton was so opposed to Burr that he ended up supporting the man running against him in his party: Thomas Jefferson. And, it is because of Hamilton's support of Jefferson that he won out over Burr. But, this decision would ultimately lead to the rising tensions between Hamilton and Burr, and because of those rising tensions, it would set Burr and Hamilton on a path that would eventually lead to Hamilton's demise.

Their feud was one that struck chords within the waves of history that are still felt today. Their arguments are still raging in our own political systems, their outlooks are still parts of the foundational basis of our two-party system, and their precedent-setting altercation in Congress over the Constitutional interpretation of Hamilton's national bank set a precedence for government expansion, much to Jefferson's dismay. Their feud not only showed us that even our Founding Fathers had difficulties agreeing with each other, but that those same people that disagreed could also pull together and see to it that things get done, such as in the case of Jefferson being elected president.

Chapter Four: Hamilton, Our Founding Father

In 1787, Hamilton was an assemblyman in the New York State Legislature. He was chosen as a delegate for the Constitutional Convention that he helped spearhead (though had very little direct influence in) by his father-in-law, Philip Schuyler. Governor George Clinton's group in the New York legislature had chosen New York's other two delegates, and both of them opposed Hamilton's goal of a strong national government. So, whenever the other two members of the New York delegation were present, they decided New York's vote time and time again. It was a tactic utilized to ensure that there were no major alterations to the Articles of Confederation, and it was something that highly frustrated Hamilton.

Early in the Convention, he made a speech. This speech proposed, among other things, a President-for-Life. Not so shockingly, it had no effect on the deliberations of the convention, and would end up being one of the reasons why Hamilton was not taken seriously among his colleagues and "peers." He proposed to have a President as well as Senators, all of whom were elected, who would serve for life. But, that life sentence was contingent upon good behavior and subject to removal if scandal or corruption ever entered the picture. This was the idea that would fuel James Madison's argument later that Hamilton was a monarchist sympathizer.

According to Madison's notes, Hamilton actually said that the "English model" was the only good idea on the subject regarding elected presidents and senators. The argument held that the King's ideals were so interwoven with his country, and passed down through generations, that he was actually above the idea of corruption. Then, Hamilton argued that Madison's definition of monarchy didn't actually hold up because the mere fact that these people would be elected demolished the definition of "monarchy."

During the convention, Hamilton constructed a draft for the Constitution based on the convention debates, however he never ended up presenting it. Nevertheless, his draft had most of the features of the final drafting of the U.S. Constitution anyway. In this personal draft, the Senate would be elected based on a proportion of its resounding population (being two-fifths the size of the House) and the president-elect and senators-elect would be appointed through complex, multistage elections. They would hold office for life, but were subject to removal for misconduct, and the President would be bestowed with the power of absolute veto. Also, in this draft, the Supreme Court would have immediate jurisdiction over all lawsuits involving the U.S., and state governors were to be appointed by the federal government.

By the end of the Convention, Hamilton was still not content with the final Constitution. But, he signed it anyway, stating that it was a great improvement over the Articles of Confederation, and he implored his fellow delegates to do the same. The other two members of the New York delegation withdrew for multiple reasons, which is why Hamilton is the only New York signer to the United States Constitution. He took a highly active part in a successful campaign for the document's ratification in New York in 1788 despite kickback from George Clinton's faction. Clinton's faction wanted to make changes to the Constitution that wrote in the concept of the state's right to secede if specific things about ratifying the Constitution failed, but Hamilton wasn't having it. During the state's convention, New Hampshire and Virginia became the ninth and tenth states to ratify the Constitution, and, eventually, New York caved out of sheer necessity.

In 1788, Hamilton served another term in what ended up being the last session of the Continental Congress while still under the Articles of Confederation. When Philip Schuyler's term was up in 1791, Aaron Burr was elected in his place. Hamilton blamed Burr for this result that he considered an abomination, and that began Hamilton's slanderous words of Burr's character and person. The two men did work together from time to time, including Hamilton's army of 1798 and the Manhattan Water Company, but neither enjoyed the company of the other, and Hamilton's tongue made sure that everyone knew it.

Hamilton recruited John Jay and James Madison to write a series of essays defending the proposed Constitution (now known as *The Federalist Papers*) and ended up making the largest contribution. Hamilton wrote 51 of the 85 essays published, supervised the entire project, and wrote under the pen name of Publius. His highlights included the science of politics, division of powers, checks and balances, and the fact that legislators needed to be represented and supported by their electors. During the project, everyone was responsible for their own areas of expertise: Jay covered foreign relations, Madison covered the history of republics and confederacies (as well as the setup and inner workings of the new government), and Hamilton covered the executive and judicial branches as well as military matters and taxation.

President George Washington appointed Hamilton as the first U.S. Secretary of the Treasury on September 11, 1789. Much of the structure of the government was worked out in those five years, and it began with the function and structure of the cabinet itself. It is said that today's modern setup of the cabinet in relation to the President was set forth by Hamilton, and that it was Hamilton that actually appointed the first "cabinet members" under President Washington. In 1791, Hamilton was elected a Fellow of the American Academy of Arts and Sciences while still Secretary of the Treasury as well as kept up with his duties at his political post, such as submitting various financial reports to Congress. Among these reports are the First Report on the Public Credit, Operations of the Act

Laying Duties on Imports, Report on a National Bank, On the
Establishment of a Mint, Report on Manufactures, and the
Report on a Plan for the Further Support of Public Credit.

Hamilton had many ideas about how the federal
government should handle their finances as well as how to stay
on top of paying off their debt, and he made sure to outline it in
every single report he ever submitted. So, the overarching point
in Hamilton's project of an administrative republic is the idea,
and establishment, of financial stability.

Hamilton resigned from office in 1795, in the wake of his
wife's miscarriage. However, before leaving his post on January
31, 1795, Hamilton submitted a *Report on a Plan for the Further
Support of Public Credit* to Congress to help curb the debt
problem. Hamilton was incredibly dissatisfied with what he saw
as the absence of a detailed and understandable plan to fix the
issue of public debt. He wanted to have new taxes passed and
have older ones ingrained as permanent, and proclaimed that
any surplus from the tax on liquor should be pledged to lower
overall public debt. His proposals ended up being included in a
bill by Congress slightly over a month after the end of his tenure
as Secretary of the Treasury. After his resignation, Hamilton
resumed his practicing of law in New York to remain closer to
his family during their turbulent and emotional time, but his
voice was never kept quiet when it came to political matters
locally.

Chapter Five: The American Revolution

Hamilton played a major role in the American Revolutionary War. In 1775, at the beginning of the war, he joined a militia company. In the early part of 1776, he raised a provincial artillery company, where he was appointed captain, and he was very good at what he did. His soldiers were always well fed and well paid, his guns were always well-maintained, and his ammunition supply never seemed to run low. It was the valor that he received while serving at this particular time that caught the attention of General Washington, and he would very quickly become his senior aide. General Washington was, at the time, the American forces' commander-in-chief, and he was proud to have a young Hamilton (only 21 years of age) standing at his side during various battles and conversations. Hamilton ended up being dispatched by Washington on countless missions to deliver and explain plans to Washington's various generals. Then, after the war, Hamilton was elected as a representative to the Congress of the Confederation from New York.

In 1775, after the first battle between American troops with the British troops at Lexington and Concord, Hamilton and many of his King's College fellow students joined a New York volunteer militia called the Corsicans. They eventually called themselves the Hearts of Oak. In the mornings, they would drill heavily in a graveyard near St. Paul's Chapel before their classes. They designed their own uniforms, and were eventually engaged in what turned out to be a successful raid while being fired on by the HMS *Asia*. They seized a cannon from the *Battery* (a public park that was riddled with cannons facing the water), and soon became an artillery unit.

Through his connections with influential New York patriots (like Alexander McDougall and John Jay), Hamilton began and trained up the New York Provincial Company of

Artillery in 1776. It boasted of sixty men, and he was elected
captain of the company. His company took part in the campaign
of 1776 around New York City, specifically at the Battle of White
Plains. Then, at the Battle of Trenton, the company was
stationed at the highest point of the town to keep German
soldiers contracted out by the British (called "hessians") pinned
in the Trenton Barracks.

Hamilton was also engaged in the Battle of Princeton on
January 3, 1777. After a setback in the beginning, Washington
rallied his troops and led them in a successful battle against the
British forces. Then, after making a brief stand, the British fell
back while others took up refuge in Nassau Hall. Hamilton
contributed and brought three massive cannons and set them up
to fire on the hall they were barricaded within. After that, some
American soldiers rushed to the front door, breaking it down to
expose the troops that had cornered themselves in. The British,
very quickly, put a white flag outside one of the windows to
signal their surrender just as the soldiers had taken the door
down. 194 British soldiers walked out of the building and laid
down their arms, and this signaled the end of the battle, with the
Americans emerging victorious.

However, before Hamilton became Washington's aide, he
was invited to become an aide to many prominent men, such as
William Alexander and Alexander McDougall. But, he declined
these invitations because he believed his best chance for
improving himself and his station in life was the glory found on
the battlefield alongside his comrades. Hamilton eventually
received an invitation to be General Washington's aide, and he
felt that it was an opportunity that he couldn't turn down. He
would end up stepping into the rank of Lieutenant Colonel, and
he took the position without a second thought.

Hamilton served four years as Washington's chief aide.
He took care of penning letters to Congress, state governors, and
the most powerful generals in the Continental Army. He helped
draft Washington's orders and letters as they were dictated to

him, and he even climbed to the point where Washington trusted him enough to issue orders from Washington without having to consult Washington in the process. Hamilton was involved in many high-level duties, such as intelligence and negotiation with senior army officers, as Washington's emissary, and earned a reputation of reliability and trustworthiness in the process. These are just a few of the many reasons why, during the war, Hamilton became close friends with many of his fellow officers that he would write to on a daily basis under the pen and dictation of Washington.

Hamilton helped at Washington's side when the British later left Philadelphia in the spring of 1778 as well as at the Battle of Monmouth in June of that same year. While assisting at Monmouth, Hamilton had his horse blatantly shot out from underneath him. He remained unharmed, however. Then, after the battle had come to a close, General Charles Lee was court-martialed for misconduct during the fight, and Hamilton ended up testifying against Lee (along with Colonel John Laurens, another one of Washington's aides). But, the after-battle drama does not stop there, because after the court-martial hearing Hamilton acted as Laurens' second in a duel initiated by Lee himself. Then, after Monmouth, Hamilton was assigned the task of tracking down Benedict Arnold.

Even with the hiccups, his time serving alongside and working for Washington ended up being one of the most educational experience of Hamilton's life. He forged the leadership skills necessary for life as a public figure, he created lasting friendships that would serve him well in his later years, and he created a strong and lasting friendship with George Washington, who would eventually appoint him as Secretary of the Treasury. His friendship with Washington helped him to solidify his political beliefs, and it molded him into the blazing figure that history books are familiar with in his latter years.

But, not everything about Hamilton's life in the military was hard work. He was a young handsome colonel, which meant that he would travel with Washington and his other assistants to visit many young women. For years, Hamilton was a huge proponent of staying single and never settling down, but he would eventually fall in love and marry Elizabeth Schuyler. The marriage between him and Miss Schuyler brought Hamilton multiple military connections and great wealth, but historians have since settled on the fact that Hamilton did love his wife despite the connections she brought along with her.

While on Washington's staff, Hamilton longed to return to active combat and command while standing alongside his comrades. As the war began to come to a close, he knew that the chances for military glory were diminishing, and he began to panic that he might not have enough time to take the path he had originally chosen to take in the first place. In February 1781, Hamilton was cautiously reprimanded by Washington, and ended up using the reprimand as an excuse to resign from his position. He asked Washington and others for a field command, and the negotiations went back and forth until early July of that same year.

But finally, on July 31, 1781, Washington gave into Hamilton's kind demands and assigned him as commander of a New York light infantry battalion. He was given this post amidst all of the planning for the assault on Yorktown, and Hamilton's command consisted of three battalions. These battalions, which were to fight alongside the allied French troops, were responsible in battling against the troops of the British Army at Yorktown. Hamilton and his battalions fought bravely and ended up taking British Redoubt No. 10 as planned out beforehand while the French took Redoubt No. 9. The French suffered heavy losses, but ended up emerging victorious. These conglomerate actions forced the British to surrender, which had a cascading impact that ended the major British military operations in North America.

However, despite all of these incredible accomplishments, this is not all that Hamilton was doing during the Revolutionary War. The first group of "draftees," or people enlisted to fight a war they did not want to fight, were African Americans. Many people, especially in the South, were afraid to arm them, but it was the dwindling enlistments of white men into the war that caused the draft of African American men. It was written that, if they fought in the war, their freedom would be exchanged for their service, and in 1775 Washington even allowed them to reenlist, should they want to. This ongoing use of African Americans in the war didn't go unprotested, with Rhode Island and many of the southern states vehemently opposing this idea. However, not all of the southern states felt that way. From the beginning, Virginia allowed African Americans to join their militias, and South Carolina was the first (and only) state to willingly enlist them before resorting to drafting them in 1781.

Alexander Hamilton was one of the major proponents of utilizing African Americans in the war, stating that, since they had always lived a life of subordination, they would make perfect soldiers. However, he highly doubted the that southerners of the country would be in agreement with that plan. However, once everything was said and done, Hamilton was a major hand in training African American soldiers to fight in the war, and was a massive voice to compensating them for their work done within it.

Hamilton had a massive career within the Revolutionary War, and the entity of his future was solidified in those young fighting years he spent alongside General Washington. His political beliefs were confirmed, he met his future wife, and he made connections that would serve him well in his political career long after his stint in the war was finished.

Chapter Six: What Alexander Hamilton Gave Us

Alexander Hamilton was very influential in the interpretation and promotion of the U.S. Constitution. He is also the founder of the nation's financial system. His other notable accomplishments are: founding the Federalist Party, the United States Coast Guard, and *The New York Post*. As if that wasn't enough, as the first U.S. Secretary of the Treasury, Hamilton was the main researcher and author of economic policies under President Washington. He is also the face of our current $10 bill.

Hamilton is widely considered the father of modern economics. As President Washington's Secretary of the Treasury, he took the lead in establishing the funding of state debt by the government as well as the creation of a national bank, a system of taxes, and ultimately he established and revived friendly trade relations with Britain.

His entire outlook on government included a strong central government, a strong commercial economy that rivaled others in the world market, a national bank, support for manufacturing within the country, and a strong military. He felt that a strong economic policy as well as being rivals in the world market would bring the budding U.S. nation up to par with many of the countries that surrounded it. He lost sleep over implementing some of these plans, and many of them were challenged by Thomas Jefferson and James Madison, who eventually formed the Federalist's opposing party. This opposing party favored strong states with roots in rural America and turned their noses up at a strong overall military in favor of individual state militias that would protect their individual states. They began a slander campaign against Hamilton, calling for eyes on the fact that he was too friendly towards

Britain and a monarchy, and favored business and banking over the welfare of the nation's people.

Some of the tariffs that Hamilton was successful in implementing were on whiskey, and domestic spirits. He set up a system that would require tailored taxes to the percentage of whiskey proof alcohol, and his plan was to equalize the tax burden by splitting the tax rate on just imported spirits between imported spirits and domestic liquor. While he still experienced some serious upheaval by the rural areas of America, he found that this option was going to be the overall favor in front of land taxes, which was something Congress had been batting around.

Not all of Hamilton's proposed taxes were a success. He attempted, when passing the tax on whiskey, to also have taxes on imported wines, coffee, and tea. However, Congress shot all of them down, stating that imposing too many taxes on goods at once could result in yet another rebellion. Hamilton was frustrated, but because of the backlash of the tax on whiskey and domestic spirits, Hamilton wrote that people could pay 60 cents by the gallon of dispensing capacity if they didn't want to fool with the complex algorithms that Hamilton was using, along with a complete tax exemption that would be made available to small stills used exclusively for domestic consumption.

But, tried as they might to have appeased the people with these taxes, it didn't quite work. Inspectors of distilleries and storehouses for spirits began to be shunned and threatened under the statements from the landowners that the inspections were intrusive, and those same inspectors also experienced moments of being tarred and feathered, blindfolded, and even whipped. Hamilton tried to calm everyone down with lowered tax rates, but it wasn't enough to stop the savage mutiny. This strong opposition to the whiskey tax, and the complications from it, erupted into the Whiskey Rebellion in 1794. Hamilton would accompany President Washington to the rebellion site, as well as being accompanied by multiple federal troops, and the site of them all cresting the hill intimidated the leaders of the rebellion to back down. To this day, it remains the cleanest rebellion in history.

Hamilton's multiple interpretations of the Constitution written about in the *Federalist Papers* still remain highly influential, and are still used in scholarly studies and court decisions today. Constitutional interpretation (the term used by all of the Founding Fathers was "constitutional *construction*") is the strict process that all legal decisions go through to figure out whether something is justified by the Constitution. Controversies, or contradictions that cannot merely be settled by just reading, usually surround whether something is consistent with, or authorized by, the Constitution. Whether it is the courts having to make a decision or a bill attempting to get passed into law, all have to go through a background check against the U.S. Constitution.

Since the Constitution is law, and the courts express law within their particular domains (and authorize statutes and other official acts), the foundations and principles of constitutional interpretation are revered as the same as judicial interpretation. Many legal scholars today recognize six main ways of interpreting the Constitution: textual, historical, functional, doctrinal, prudential, equitable, and natural. This entire foundation was laid out in Hamilton's *Federalist Papers,* and his arguments against Jefferson in Congress laid the first precedent where constitutional interpretation was something to be debated and argued over.

Even though the Constitution is pretty ambiguous in terms of the exact percentage in balance of power between national and state governments, Hamilton always took the side of greater federal power, even if it was at the expense of the states. As Secretary of the Treasury, he established the country's first national bank, lending him more economic credit for the generations to come. He justified the creation of this bank under Congress's written constitutional power to issue and distribute currency, regulate commerce, and do anything else that would be "necessary and proper" to make sure that the provisions of the Constitution were held to the utmost extent.

Jefferson opposed, taking a much a stricter view of the Constitution. He picked apart the text carefully, and when he did, he found no specific authorization for a national bank. This controversy that raged for many months was finally settled by the Supreme Court in *McCulloch v. Maryland*, which sided with Hamilton's view. This was the first ever precedent of granting the federal government expanded powers, broadening its reach within its own nation.

Hamilton's policies as Secretary of the Treasury, as well as his written and oral interpretations of the U.S. Constitution, still greatly affect and influence the United States government today. His interpretation of the Necessary and Proper Clause set multiple precedents in regards to federal authority that are still used by courts today, and are even considered one of the higher authorities on constitutional interpretation. Hamilton was so revered that a prominent French diplomat, Charles Maurice de Talleyrand, wrote that he considered the three greatest men of their era to be Napoleon, Fox, and Hamilton. He then went on to state that, if he had to choose between the three, that he would give the award to Hamilton without hesitation.

Hamilton is also attributed to founding the Revenue Marine, which is what would evolve into our modern day Coast Guard. However, it didn't initially start as a search-and-rescue service. The original coast guard was founded on August 4, 1790, and was tasked with executing seaport customs services. The Revenue Marine, eventually renamed to the Revenue Cutter Service, also was tasked with the "much smaller" task of providing aid for the protection of lives and goods/property at sea.

However, it isn't until 1915 that the coast guard would have the name bestowed upon it that we now know today. During that year, the Department of the Treasury ended up merging the Revenue Cutter Service with many different maritime venues: The Bureau of Navigation, the Steamboat Inspection Service, the Lighthouse Service, and the Lifesaving Service. It has since been recognized as an armed force, like the U.S. Army and the U.S. Navy, and as a result of that categorization, the U.S. Coast Guard has played a role in every war since its inception.

Alexander Hamilton gave the molding United States a great deal that we still utilize to this very day. His interpretation of the Constitution is foundationally used in courtrooms, his economic policies still ring tried and true today in the U.S. world marketplace, and even the controversies such as rural farmers versus big business and bankers still rage on today because of Hamilton's ways of thinking. His *Federalist Papers* helped to kick-start a revolution that spun his web of historical context throughout his life, and his relationship that he grew with President George Washington can be backtracked all the way into his early twenties when Hamilton was just a young soldier. Hamilton's creation of the Revenue Marine might have been to simply help him keep track of goods that came into ports, but it blossomed into something I don't think even he could have seen coming.

No matter how you feel about the politics of Hamilton, his voice and his beliefs established a massive side to this two-party system that echoes throughout the halls of our federal government today, and it is because of him and his economic policies that the growing U.S. saw the type of success in the world market that it did at such a young age.

Chapter Seven: The Scandals of Hamilton

No prominent figure within history is without scandal, and that includes our own Alexander Hamilton. From the beginning, when he was birthed out of wedlock, to the end, when he was dealt a fatal gunshot wound in a duel against Aaron Burr, his life has consistently held a level of scandal that is rivaled only by some of our nation's greatest scandals in the last two decades. One of those scandals? It was none other than the first sex scandal ever to be publicized by the public.

In the summer of 1797, Hamilton became the first American politician to be found guilty of a sex scandal and chastised for it. Six years prior, Hamilton, clocking in at a young 34 years of age, started an affair with a woman by the name of Maria Reynolds, who was only 23 years of age. According to Hamilton's spokesperson, Maria actually approached him at his house in Philadelphia and claimed that her husband, James Reynolds, had abandoned her. She expressed wishes to return to her relatives in New York, but didn't have the financial means to do so. Hamilton, in return, retrieved her address and delivered her $30 personally in order to help her get home. According to the account, she led him into her bedroom and conversation quickly turned into something different. The two began a secret affair that lasted the better part of a year before parting ways for unknown reasons.

Over the course of that year, while the two of them were "shacking up," James Reynolds was, apparently, fully aware of his wife's infidelity. In actuality, he was in continuous support of it with the sole purpose to blackmail Hamilton for more money. Back in these times, the common practice for infidelities such as this one was that the wronged husband had the opportunity to seek retribution in a pistol duel. However, Reynolds realized how much Hamilton had to lose if the scandal came to light in the eyes of the public, so he settled on "monetary compensation." After the first request of $1000.00, to which Hamilton complied quite quickly, Reynolds actually prostituted his wife out to gain more money from Hamilton. Reynolds would "invite" Hamilton to strike up his visits with Miss Reynolds "as a friend," only to then turn around and blackmail Hamilton for money after their solicited visits.

Before everything was said and done, the blackmail payments totaled over $1300. Hamilton, at this point, was probably aware of both James and Maria's involvement, and it was probably this revelation (along with the growing risk involved and the hole it was burning in his wallet) that prompted Hamilton to request an end to the entire situation.

We are well aware, at this point, of Hamilton's swirling controversial political time. From his feud with Thomas Jefferson to his lofty interpretations of government, Hamilton found people questioning him and cursing him with every turn he made as Secretary of the Treasury. However, when Hamilton resigned in 1795, it didn't remove him from the public life. With resuming his law practice, he remained close to Washington as an advisor and friend. Hamilton continued to influence Washington by aiding him in the composition of Washington's Farewell Address. Hamilton drafted his speeches, one-by-one and side-by-side, until the exact one that Washington wanted to make had finally appeared. Many people were incredibly upset that a man who no longer held a governmental position still had a great influence on their President, and it earned him quite a bit of backlash.

In the election of 1796, that backlash was dubiously heard. Under the Constitution as it stood then, the process went like this: each one of the presidential electors had two votes a piece, and they were required to cast those two votes for different men. The one who received the most votes would become President, and the one who acquired the second-most votes would be Vice President. The Federalists, hating this way of electing their two most important seats in office, planned to deal with it by having all of their electors vote for John Adams, Washington's Vice President. The issue? Adams wholly resented Hamilton's influence on Washington.

Adams thought that Hamilton was overambitious in his public life and scandalous in his private life, and Hamilton made sure to fire back. He compared Adams in a contrasting light to Washington, and stated that he was too emotionally unstable to be President. Hamilton would then take the election as an opportunity to try and plot. His plan required an intricate set of details: he would urge all of the northern electors to vote for Adams and Pinckney under the argument that no one wanted Jefferson in the running, but he then would cooperate with Edward Rutledge so that South Carolina's electors would vote for Jefferson and Pinckney.

If all of this worked, Pinckney would pull ahead with more votes than Adams, which meant that Pinckney would become President and Adams would remain Vice President. However, the complicated plan of deception didn't work. The Federalists found out about his plan, so the northern Federalists voted for Adams and *not* for Pinckney. In the end, it resulted in Jefferson becoming Vice President and John Adams being elected president, much to Hamilton's public dismay.

Then, scandal struck his life again. During the gubernatorial elections of 1804 in New York, Hamilton assisted Morgan Lewis quite a bit, which ended up winning him the election over Aaron Burr. After this election, the *Albany Register* published a batch of letters written by Charles D. Cooper. They talked about Hamilton's stark opposition to Burr and made claims that Hamilton had expressed a disgusting opinion of Burr at a dinner party. Burr read about the attack on his honor and swiftly demanded an apology in the form of a letter from Hamilton.

In response, Hamilton wrote a letter refusing to apologize because he claimed he couldn't recall the instance of insulting

Burr. After multiple attempts to reconcile, a duel was arranged through go-to men for June 27, 1804. Before the duel, Hamilton penned a defense of his decision to duel while, at the same time, expressed intent to intentionally botch his shot. Hamilton cited his roles of being a father as well as husband and explained that his death would put his own family's welfare at risk. He also talked about his creditors and how his absence would put them in jeopardy, as well as how this duel compromised his moral and religious stances.

But, he also stated that he felt that it was impossible to avoid because of Burr's behavior prior to the duel, despite the "fact" that Hamilton couldn't recall the instances that he had insulted Burr. He intended to accept the duel against Burr and toss aside his pride in order to justice to the public's implied moral codes.

The duel began the morning of July 11, 1804, and took place along the west bank of the Hudson River on a rocky ledge located in Weehawken, New Jersey. After the seconds, elected by Burr and Hamilton respectively, measured the paces, Hamilton raised his pistol and had to wear his glasses so that he could see. It is said that Hamilton refused a hairspring set of dueling pistols that was offered to him by Nathaniel Pendleton. Those hairsprings would have made pulling the trigger easier, and it might have saved his life in the process, had he chosen to utilize them.

Vice President Burr shot Hamilton and delivered a fatal shot. Hamilton's shot broke a tree branch directly above Burr's head, and it is said that Hamilton's gun was the second to fire, rather than the first. Even after triangulating the shots after the duel was over, they still couldn't even determine from what angle Hamilton fired, lending more evidence to the fact that he likely fired his gun as he was tumbling backwards from the bullet from Burr's gun. Burr's shot hit Hamilton square in the lower abdomen, just above his right hip. The bullet ended up ricocheting off Hamilton's third false rib, fractured it, and caused considerable damage to his internal organs, especially his liver and diaphragm. Then, after all of that damage was done, the bullet lodged in his second lumbar vertebra, paralyzing him.

Hamilton was well aware that he had been mortally wounded, and, after the duel, was ferried to William Bayard Jr.'s Greenwich Village home. After many final visits from his family and friends (and a great deal of suffering) Alexander Hamilton died the next day on July 12, 1804, at Bayard's home.

Hamilton's life was drenched in scandal, controversy, and questions. From his scandalous birth and abandonment of his parents to the constant political feud between him and Jefferson, it was no wonder that the scandal followed him once he resigned from his political life as well. His dedication to his country and his government played a massive role in his involvement with politics even after he resumed practicing law, and he died doing exactly what it was that all of our Founding Fathers were doing with their lives: defending their strong opinions on the foundations of our government during a time when this country was nothing but a child in rearing. His legacy, both good and bad, carry him throughout history as one of the most prevalent figures in our country's development.

Chapter Eight: His Legacy

Alexander Hamilton had a massive influence on the development of America's economic theories, political institutions, and many of its public policies during its inception. He is known for his personality, his politics, and his valuable contributions to constitutional interpretation.

His political ideals and the things that he saw as of the utmost importance form many of the foundations of one of America's two major political parties, and if it wasn't for the controversy that surrounded his ideals, we probably would have seen two different parties emerge at all. It wasn't just his political opinions that garnered his reputation, it was the feuds (and the eventual rise of another political party) that puts him into the history books as one of the most influential men in America's history.

His greatest contribution, by far, are his *Federalist Papers*. He wrote 51 of the 86 written and published, and within them houses a theory of politics that is deeply-seated in stark realism. In his idea of foreign affairs, he combined the virtue of honor and the appreciation of power with national character. He sought to have peaceful trade relations with country that were once considered enemies, and he saw massive potential in the worldwide market that was hard to sell to those who couldn't see past the wars.

In his ideal economy, Hamilton proposed a national bank that would aid the federal government in superseding the debts of the states and felt that tariffs were the way to go when acquiring money for operating costs of the federal government. He felt that everyone residing in a country had a duty to aid their government and its officials in their day-to-day financial goings on, and this was what brought the Hamilton-Jefferson feud to a head. To this day, that feud is one of the starkest in America's history. Jefferson felt that a central government that had little influence in the general financial market and a country that was more focused around rural America and its farmers was the way to go, and Hamilton accused him of living in the present instead of looking towards the future. This feud would continue through the courts as he battled Jefferson on constitutional interpretation of a national bank, and would ultimately win out, much to Jefferson's dismay.

Hamilton saw the regulation of the nation's debt as a way to create monetary flow to other things the budding country would need, such as means for regulating currency and funding a national military. His tax system was, by far, the most unpopular thing that was developed, and the tax on whiskey that he enacted would end up leading to the Whiskey Rebellion, where we would see the first moment in America's history where the government utilized military force in order to get its citizens to stand down. That tactic is still used in courtrooms today to justify the same action, such as the controversy with protests at the Dakota Pipeline in 2016.

Hamilton would be aghast at the debt our country has today. He believed that, while debt for a growing nation was unavoidable, that it should also remain small and manageable. Getting past his tax reforms, this was the undergird of his entire economic plan. He knew that this would ensure the nation a credit rating equal to those in Europe and earn them a spot in the global market, and that is where his overall financial plan was headed when he was Secretary of the Treasury.

However, Hamilton's theory of constitutional government is the epitome of what he left behind in terms of political theory. He supported a separation of powers between the emerging branches of government and wholly adopted a belief in the system of checks and balances. Hamilton didn't advocate for a monarchy, even though such rumors were perpetrated by Jefferson, but he did favor a mixed government. He even wrote down in his own draft of the U.S. Constitution that the executive should have the independence of a monarch but be held accountable by a system of checks and balances. His understanding of judicial power, however skewed, ended up helping this nation form the basis for the judicial branch of government, who also works under Hamilton's proposed system of checks and balances. He believed that the President needed to be shielded from the passions of the people in order to uphold the national interest, and he felt that a judiciary system would be able to take that burden from the President and uphold the law above all else, no matter what was presented to them.

However, Hamilton's legacy isn't all positive. Some of his policies were wholly turned down, such as electing people into political office for life, and his personal life was riddled with controversy, such as his sordid sexual affair with Maria Reynolds and his eventual murder by Aaron Burr in a state-sanctioned duel that delivered a fatal wound to his abdomen.

However peppered his life was with scandal, the contributions that he made to our budding nation when he was alive are priceless. He argued his political ideals with incredible energy, and it was that energy and bull-headedness that he displayed in his everyday life that made him the force that he was. He was not only a smart man, he also knew when he needed to bite down on his lower lip and dig his heels in, such as in the ratification of the U.S. Constitution. Even though he signed a document he wasn't completely in agreement with, no one worked harder than him in various states in order to get the state governments to agree and vote in its favor.

Hamilton's eventually-won interpretation of the "necessary and proper" clause is, arguably, the most important contribution to the rest of America's history that we have. It set a precedence not only for Congress's power, but also for extending the reach of the federal government. Many believed that this clause left little to no room to limit Congress's power, but what it does actually is it requires statesmen to utilize the overall virtue of prudence. It keeps the states in their place by giving the federal government means to override any law they pass and any rebellion that might upheave that threatens the fabric of the nation. This clause, of course, leans on the existence of talented and transparent public officers, but the clause was necessary. Not only does our federal government have checks and balances, but under this argument that he won for the "necessary and proper" clause, the state governments now have a check with the federal government as well.

Hamilton's contribution to the political thoughts, theories, and ideologies of the United States of America is significant. His contributions, along with those who bucked against him, go down in history as the men that helped establish the foundations of our current government, economic policies, and military. Hamilton is not only responsible for everything that has been talked about already, but he is also responsible for establishing the Revenue Cutter Service, which would eventually merge with several other maritime organizations to form what we now call our U.S. Coast Guard. His system of checks and balances that he fleshed out wholly became the basis for how our current government operates and keeps itself balanced, and his constitutional interpretation is still reverberated along the walls of courtrooms today as we argue topics of modern importance on foundations that were set several centuries ago.

Alexander Hamilton gave this country many tools that it needed in order to create its foundation. Peppered with scandal and killed on the field in a duel, Hamilton's life began in scandalous beginnings and ended in such as well. But, between those humble beginnings and that not-so-humble end, Hamilton influenced our government, our judicial system, our Constitution, and our economic system in a way no other person would. His strong suit might not have been in strict political theories, but it was in establishing the economics that would enable the U.S. to compete on the world market, hold its citizens accountable for helping the government monetarily regulate itself, and give voice to many people who wanted to see their budding nation progress from rural America into industrial America.

Conclusion

Thanks again for taking the time to read this book!

You should now have a good understanding of Alexander Hamilton life, and his many incredible contributions to the development of the United States of America as we know it today.

If you enjoyed this book, please take the time to leave me a review on Amazon. I appreciate your honest feedback, and it really helps me to continue producing high quality books.